Susan (handwritten)

Workbook

For

Sanjay Gupta's

Keep Sharp

Build A Better Brain At Any Age

Robin Reads

Table of Contents

About The Book 1

About The Workbook 4

Part One – Meet the Brain 7

Chapter One – Your Black Box....................... 7

Chapter Two – Cognitive Decline 14

Chapter Three – Debunking Myths............... 25

Part Two – Maintaining a Healthy Brain ... 34

Chapter Four – Why Movement is Important 34

Chapter Five – Keep The Brain Active........... 44

Chapter Six – Sleep and Relaxation.............. 51

Chapter Seven – Eating for Brain Health...... 61

Chapter Eight - The People Connection........ 71

Chapter Nine – 12 Weeks to A Sharper You.. 77

Part Three – The Diagnosis and After 86

Chapter 10 – What to Do 86

Chapter 11 – Arranging Support and Care ... 96

Conclusion 103

Addendum 104

About The Book

It is a fact that many people fear memory loss as they get older. In his book, "Keep Sharp: Build a Better Brain at Any Age", Dr Sanjay Gupta debunks the myth that memory loss is a "preordained part of aging". He says that once you understand why your brain works the way it does, you can have a greater influence on its memory and thinking abilities than you realize.

Although scientists have not yet discovered a means of curing cognitive decline related to diseases such as Alzheimer's, we now have a better understanding of how the brain works. We can use this understanding to devise strategies to help us optimize our brain, improve its functionality and ward off brain illnesses related to age.

Throughout the book, Dr Gupta shares much of the information he gleaned from extensive research around cognitive degeneration from various sources. Some of these sources from around the world include well known studies, scientists, researchers, colleagues, other cultures, and his own observations.

In the Introduction to his book, Sanjay Gupta tells us why he became fixated on learning more about the brain. When he was thirteen years old his grandfather had a stroke and he witnessed his grandfather's brain function go through a rapid change/decline. Sanjay started researching more about how the brain functioned and became fascinated with the subject of memory.

Much later, while he was at medical school, he learned that our brain cells are not fixed, they continue to grow and regenerate. After he completed his neurosurgery training, he became convinced that it is possible for us to make our brains "better, faster, fitter", and "sharper".

His book focuses not on improving one's intelligence or IQ, but rather on how we can generate new brain cells and make the ones we already have work more efficiently. He aims to teach resilience and how to nurture one's brain with the goal of protecting against cognitive decline and diseases such as Alzheimer's and dementia. Much of his advice focuses on lifestyle changes; nutrition, exercise, sleeping habits, and with whom we socialize.

The book is divided into 3 parts.

In part one of the book, Gupta takes us through the workings of the brain. We get to explore the most mysterious of our organs and learn how memory works. Here Gupta takes the opportunity to debunk some long-held beliefs about aging and cognitive decline and talks about how the brain is capable of being remodeled and rewired and how it can grow.

In part 2 he provides practical strategies and a 12-week program to follow if we want to learn how to protect our brain and keep it sharp as we age. He says one does not have to wait to be diagnosed before implementing protective measures to keep one's brain sharp. He suggests ways to build a better brain at any age and how to maximize brain health.

Part 3 of the book delves into the stress and problems that caregivers encounter while caring for their loved ones who have Alzheimer's. Information and resources are provided about health care facilities and assisted living options for the elderly diagnosed with Alzheimer's or dementia. Some of these facilities do come with their own issues apart from the cost factor and many people, especially women of the family, end up caring for their relatives at home.

The symptoms of brain-related illnesses can appear decades before diagnosis, therefore it is important for younger generations to care for their brain health to prevent the possibility of future cognitive decline.

About The Workbook

Some of you who pick up this workbook may already have read Dr. Sanjay Gupta's original book. For these folks, this workbook will be beneficial in assisting you to put into practice the ideas from his book.

For those who have not read the original book, we have included an excellent chapter by chapter summary of Keep Sharp. If you have already read the book, these detailed summaries will also help you remember the contents of the original book and serve as a quick reference guide.

The workbook is designed to be used as a companion to the original book. Each chapter contains a detailed summary, key takeaways, and a series of activities. The activities are designed to apply the ideas and suggestions from the original book to your own life in a practical and meaningful way.

This workbook aims to help you engage with the issues raised by Sanjay Gupta on a more personal level. In doing so, we hope you will gain a better understanding of your brain and how to keep it healthy and sharp. You will put Dr. Gupta's ideas into practice to develop a more "resilient" brain to deal with the trials of daily life. To maintain a healthy brain, you must make healthy decisions.

To get the full benefits of this workbook you will need to set aside some quiet time to think and reflect on the questions and complete the activities.

More on Dr Sanjay Gupta

Well-known CNN chief medical correspondent and neurosurgeon, Dr Sanjay Gupta, also hosts the acclaimed podcast Coronavirus: Fact vs Fiction. He is the best-selling author of two other non-fiction books, Chasing Life, Chasing Death, and Monday Mornings.

Dr Gupta has received multiple Emmy and Peabody awards, as well as the DuPont Award for his work. He was also elected to the National Academy of Medicine in 2019, one of the highest honors in the medical field.

Currently, Dr Gupta lives in Atlanta, USA, with his family, where he works as an associate professor of neurosurgery at the Emory University School of Medicine. He also serves as associate chief of neurosurgery at Grady Memorial Hospital.

His many years of work in the field of neurosurgery and medical research have led him write a comprehensive book about brain functions and cognitive decline. He has traveled the world to learn more about neurological diseases.

Dr Gupta wholeheartedly believes that prevention and early intervention can address the issue of brain decline, and that understanding your brain can help you build a more resilient and sharper brain.

He says: "The brain can be continuously and consistently enriched throughout your life no matter your age or access to resources."

Part One – Meet the Brain

Chapter One – Your Black Box

Summary

Your brain – the most complex organ. According to scientists, the brain is the most complex thing to have been discovered. Despite having studied this organ for many years, neuroscientists and researchers have still not fully tapped into everything this remarkable organ offers.

However, your brain is not a complete mystery box. Through the field of neuroscience, researchers have and are continuing to develop a deeper understanding of the brain's areas and connections.

In Chapter 1 of Keep Sharp, Dr Gupta gives us some interesting facts about our brain so that we can gain a better understanding of how it works. Did you know?

- The average weight of the human brain is around 3.3 pounds
- It is roughly about 2.5 percent of an average person's body weight

- The brain uses up 20 percent of the total blood and oxygen produced by our bodies
- It does not have a fixed memory capacity like a computer
- The cortex which is the outer layer of the brain allows us to perform more sophisticated tasks than animals
- It consists of about 100 billion brain cells (neurons) and billions of nerve fibers
- The neurons are linked by connections called synapses which is the main reason why we are able to remember, to form language, to be creative, to think abstractly, to feel emotions, to make decisions, to plan, to communicate our intentions, to coordinate dance moves, to solve complex problems, to sense things, to analyze information and so on

EXEC FUNCTION

- The part of our brains that includes our consciousness has still not been precisely located
- Because the brain is about 73 percent water, just 2 percent of dehydration can affect cognitive skills such as memory and attention

HYDRATE

- The human brain only reaches full maturity at around the age of twenty-five
- Brain information can travel as fast as 250miles per hour
- The part of the brain that is considered the memory center is called the hippocampus. Shrinkage of the hippocampus results in shrinkage of memory.

In the past, many believed that we are born with a certain number of neurons and that as we age our brain declines. But according to Dr Gupta, our brains are not static -they are alive. We can grow new brain cells (neurogenesis) and build new connections. The brain can heal and rehabilitate itself and re-establish connections even after injury (neuroplasticity).

Our brains grow and learn and change throughout our lives. Different areas of the brain develop at a different pace and at different stages in our lives. Therefore, an adult can, for instance, solve a problem faster and differently as compared to a child. Each part of our brain serves a specific purpose that links together to function smoothly.

Memory

Memory is a cognitive function and so is writing, reading, thinking, and performing everyday tasks among others. These WRITING are recognized as higher brain functions. Of all of these, memory is the most recognized. It serves as the foundation for all learning. It is in our memories that we store and process knowledge.

Our memories are constantly changing. It is not static as is commonly thought. Every time we take in new information and interpret this information, our memories change. Previously stored information can be altered as we encounter new information.

Our memory is more complex than we think and Dr Gupta suggests that the more we understand our memories, the more inspired we will be to improve them.

Memory is a "brain-wide active collaboration", that is, it is not confined to any one area of the brain. It comprises a network of systems and each of these systems plays its own role in creating, storing, and recalling information. These systems work together (synchronicity) to provide cohesive thought. It's almost like the pieces of a puzzle that must come together to make sense.

Memory building happens in three phases:

Encoding – at this stage you start creating a memory based on your first perceptions or impressions of a situation or a person – what you see feel and hear (sensory memory).

Storage – our memories work on two levels: short-term memory and long-term memory. Sensory memory moves into your short-term memory to be stored for a certain period. To be able to retain and recall information it must be transferred from your short-term memory (linked to the hippocampus) to your long-term memory (linked to the outer layers of your brain, your cortex). Things like sleep deprivation and alcohol can interrupt the process of transferring a memory from short term to long term.

Hrs of sleep?

Retrieval – this is the process of calling up a memory – moving it from an unconscious level to your conscious mind.

Sometimes our retrieval systems don't work so well and we say we have a bad or poor memory. This happens for example in instances where you forget a person's name or you simply cannot recall a word you usually use. Dr Gupta says that those kinds of memory lapses can "easily be rectified by sharpening your memory skills for that particular weakness" using certain focused techniques.

As we age memory speed and accuracy naturally begin to slip but Dr Gupta believes that this is not inevitable with age. There are certain things we can do to maintain and sharpen our ability to remember. In the next chapter, we take a closer look at what is cognitive decline and whether it can be reversed.

Key Insights from this Chapter

1. The brain is less of a mystery than we think, despite its complexity.

2. The neurons in your brain continue to grow and learn as you get older.

3. The hippocampus (the center of your memory) shrinks a tiny bit per year. Shrinkage varies according to an individual's lifestyle choices.

4. Memory lapses are normal and can be rectified.

Identify Related Issues

*25%*1. How much do you know about your brain and its health?

*Yes*2. Do you find yourself forgetting more as you get older?

*Yes*3. Is it harder for you to learn new things?

*Yes*4. Do you want to learn more about memory and cognitive decline?

Goals You Want to Achieve

1. I want to learn more about my brain so I can get a better understanding of it.

2. I want to learn how to keep my mind focused and sharp.

3. I want to protect my mind from decline as I age.

Your Plan of Action

1. Make it a point to do some online research to learn more about the brain.

2. Assess whether there have been changes in my memory as I have aged. For instance, have I become more forgetful?

   WALKING INTO ROOM
   CAN'T FIND WHERE I PUT THINGS

3. Engage in discussions with my circle about mental health.

Action Checklist

1. Do I have a better understanding of the brain?

2. Do I have a clearer understanding of what is a myth and what is a fact regarding the brain?

    a. Can you list at least 3 important facts about the brain that you did not know before?

    ELASTIC
    HIPPOCAMPUS
    - MEMORY
    USES 20% BODIES OXYGEN & BLOOD

    b. What is one myth that you believed about the brain that you now know is not true?

    EITHER RIGHT OR LEFT BRAINED

3. Learn more about how memory works and how it may decline. Read books or research online. Speak to other people.

13

Chapter Two – Cognitive Decline

Summary

When a loved one starts to show signs of mental decline, it is agonizing for family members to watch this process. For some with the illness, it is a long-drawn-out process, while for others the illness can be fast.

What exactly is cognitive decline and how does it start? What can you do to help a family member?

Mental decline often starts with little slips of memory loss and gradually progresses into more obvious symptoms with the person withdrawing more. Family members often want to know how it started, what caused the decline; was it depression or a lack of exercise or, nutritional deficiencies for instance?

According to Dr. Gupta, there is no easy answer to these questions. We still don't know what can exactly trigger cognitive decline. It could be a single factor or multiple factors. There are many theories about this, but no definite answers yet.

What has become clear from various studies though is that decline can begin years before the symptoms emerge. Most people only become concerned about mental decline after the age of fifty. But because it can start much earlier, Dr. Gupta encourages younger generations to start looking at what they can do now to prevent cognitive decline from happening later.

Researchers have noted that what causes cognitive decline in one person is not necessarily what causes it in another person. Despite this, says Dr. Gupta, there are still strategies we can use to reduce our risk for decline.

In the second chapter of his book, he goes into detail about what happens in the brain of someone with Alzheimer's. As we mentioned earlier, Alzheimer's is one of the illnesses that is a result of cognitive decline and it is on the rise globally. Much of the treatment for this disease has so far been based on amyloids, more precisely beta-amyloids.

What are amyloids and beta-amyloids?

They refer to "plaques of sticky protein that accumulate in the brain and destroy those essential synapses that allow brain cells to communicate". It was believed that amyloid cascade, i.e., the accumulation of plaques around the brain cells, is what caused Alzheimer's. But scientists are not clear about how this happens. Many treatments for Alzheimer's have been based on trying to get rid of these plaques. But they have not worked in clinical trials.

Causes of Cognitive Decline

The amyloid theory is only a single culprit and as it is becoming more known now, cognitive decline can be triggered by more than one factor. Especially since it has been found that some people whose brains have a lot of this plaque do not show any signs of cognitive decline. Dr. Gupta talks about this in more detail later where he discusses the concept of "resilient brains".

Research is considering triggers such as genetics, aging, injury, exposure to harmful chemicals in the air, nutrient deficiencies, infections or, even prolonged metabolic dysfunction. All of these can cause damage to the brain due to inflammation. Most of the theories about brain decline center around inflammation.

Apart from the amyloid theory, Gupta talks about a few other potential ways that the brain can break down.

Neurofibrillary tangles and Tau proteins

Tau proteins are needed for the stability and survival of brain cells. While amyloid plaques accumulate outside brain cells, tau proteins are found inside brain cells. They help brain cells to communicate with each other. When these proteins undergo chemical changes, they become tangled and can no longer function well. They have been implicated in the cause of degenerative brain diseases such as CTE (Chronic traumatic encephalopathy), an illness due to head injury often caused by blows to the head and usually experienced by football players and boxers.

Tangles and Prions

Another type of protein one finds in the brain is known as prions. These can trigger tau and beta-amyloid proteins to tangle (fold abnormally). A common disease associated with prions is "mad cow disease" which one gets from infected meat products.

Blood flow

It has been found that plaques and even tangles occur more frequently in people with advanced vascular diseases. Blood flow to the brain is extremely important as brain function can be significantly impacted when its blood flow system is not working as well as it should. Factors such as smoking and high levels of cholesterol affect the blood flow system. High blood pressure is another factor that can cause people to be more vulnerable to developing Alzheimer's. High blood pressure can damage the arteries leading to the brain.

Metabolic Syndrome

It is estimated that many adults, particularly those over sixty have a combination of health conditions known as metabolic syndrome. These include high blood pressure, obesity, too much bad cholesterol, insulin resistance or, type 2 diabetes. Some researchers believe that insulin resistance or deficiency plays a big role in the cognitive decline that leads to Alzheimer's. Weight gain is another major factor that has been looked at. Studies show that people with a high level of abdominal fat exhibited an increased risk of dementia. Unhealthy weight gain has metabolic consequences that put the brain at risk for cognitive decline.

Toxic substances

Can exposure to chemicals we encounter in our daily lives such as pesticides result in brain abnormalities? Researchers are still working on this question. They have found that certain neurotoxins can cause amyloid plaque and tau tangles which would make them a consequence of Alzheimer's, not a cause. An amino acid known as L-serine was developed to replace one of the building blocks of these proteins. L-serine is a widely available over-the-counter supplement. Studies are showing that it can halt the progression of Alzheimer's in vervet monkeys and human trials are currently being conducted.

Infections

Diseases such as Lyme disease, the herpes virus, syphilis and, rabies can have neurological effects. Studies are being conducted to verify whether the body's reaction to these infections can result in brain decline. Not everyone who has a brain infection though develops Alzheimer's and more work is needed on this theory.

Chronic inflammation

Chronic inflammation, associated with aging, can increase one's risk of dementia and is related to diabetes and vascular diseases. It is also possibly related to other brain-related illnesses such as depression and Alzheimer's.

Aging

Normal aging can cause degeneration of your brain's synapses. Our brains begin to age in our mid-twenties and deterioration can begin as early as our thirties. The hippocampus shrinks after age 40. This shrinkage however varies from individual to individual depending on various factors. These factors include the lifestyle choices we make, our genetic predispositions, underlying medical conditions and, environmental factors. Due to all of these and other factors, we cannot conclude definitively that aging alone causes brain degeneration.

Types of Dementia

The term dementia covers a range of cognitive decline disorders from MCI to severe dementia all of which have an impact on memory or communication or thinking functions. Alzheimer's is one type of dementia. It is the most common form, accounting for "60-80 percent" of dementia cases and affects "one in nine Americans aged sixty-five and older". It is the "sixth leading cause of death in the United States".

Mild cognitive Impairment (MCI) is often the beginning stage of dementia and causes a slight decline in memory function. Not everyone with MCI ends up with severe dementia.

Another type of dementia is vascular dementia which is caused by impaired blood supply to the brain. Other types are dementia with Lewy Bodies (caused by abnormal deposits of a protein called alpha-synuclein in the brain) which affects one in every five patients who have been diagnosed with dementia (symptoms are like Parkinson's) and Frontotemporal Lobar Dementia which is also known as Picks' disease, triggered by gradual nerve loss, early signs of which are changes in personality and behavior.

Normal Memory Lapses

Not all memory problems are a sign of cognitive decline. There are six types of memory lapses that are normal and should not be cause for worry. These are:

- Absentmindedness – this is quite common and is due to a general lack of focus or attention. For example, when you walk into the house and put your keys down somewhere and you later forget where you put them. This is because you just set them down absentmindedly. You were not focused on the task.
- Blocking – when several memories crowd together the retrieval button gets jammed making it a bit frustrating when you can't recall something that you know you know. It's that situation where the answer is just on the tip of your lips but you can't nail it down.
- Scrambling – when you confuse little details about something due to a glitch in your hippocampus which

results in incorrectly recording all details of an event when it happened.

- Fading away – some of our memories tend to fade away when we don't recall them often which is quite normal. The brain cleans out unused or older memories to make room for new ones.
- Struggling for retrieval – similar to absentmindedness. As we age, we tend to forget things like a person's name after we met them for the first time. Repeating this type of new information can help store it better in our short-term memories.
- Muddled multitasking – as we get older it takes a bit more effort for the brain to focus again after an interruption and we find that we are not as good at multitasking as we once were.

Since there is no definitive way to diagnose Alzheimer's like you can, for instance heart disease, it is not uncommon for people to be diagnosed with it when they don't have it. Some people can reverse their cognitive decline even though they have been diagnosed with Alzheimer's because they never actually had it in the first place.

If you have not been diagnosed with definitive Alzheimer's but experience cognitive decline, there are things you can do to reverse the decline. Neurologist and neuroscientist, Dr. Majid Fotuhi believes that with comprehensive brain fitness programs that focus on lifestyle changes to modify risk factors such as diabetes, obesity, vascular disorders, anxiety, etc., one can encourage brain growth.

Putting your brain first

If you focus on your brain health you can optimize its performance. When your brain is healthy you make healthy decisions that affect other areas of your life – a healthy body, healthy heart, a sense of confidence, making smarter decisions which can result in better relationships and a better financial future. In the next chapters, we look at what happens when we make brain health a priority.

Key Insights from this Chapter

1. Multiple factors can trigger cognitive decline.

2. Not all memory lapses are a sign of cognitive decline.

3. Cognitive decline can be reversed if we pay more attention to brain health.

Identify Related Issues

1. Have you noticed any lapses in your memory?

2. Are there any people in your life who have been diagnosed with dementia or Alzheimer's disease?

3. Reflecting on the last few years, what have you been doing to help maintain your brain to keep it in top shape?

Goals You Want to Achieve

1. Pay more attention to and keep an eye out for cognitive decline in me and my family members.

2. Take an audit of the current lifestyle and see if it truly supports brain health.

Your Plan of Action

1. Talk to close friends and family members openly about cognitive decline and any early signs of dementia.

2. Do a self-assessment check on my brain health.

Action Checklist

How healthy is my brain

Take a look at the following markers to see which apply to you.

N1. Do you smoke currently or actually have had a history of smoking?

N2. Are you currently overweight?

N3. Is alcohol abuse a part of your life?

4. Do you have very little exercise in a week? (less than 3 hours of exercise in a week that gets your heart pumping fast. Strolling doesn't count)
5. Is your diet rich in processed foods that are chockful of sugars and hydrogenated fats?
6. Have you actually been diagnosed with cognitive issues or brain related illnesses?
7. Does your daily life lack social engagement with others?
8. In your daily routine, are you required to think deep and think actively? It can be in the form of playing complex thinking games or learning something new.
9. Does your family have a history of Alzheimer's disease?
10. Are you experiencing poor sleep patterns or have trouble getting a good night's rest?

The more "Yes-es" you have to the above questions, the more likely it is that your brain might experience cognitive decline.

In the following chapters, you will read about and put into practice potential solutions to maintain or improve brain health.

Even if you only answered yes to a couple of questions you can still benefit from learning to take care of your brain from today.

Volley Tues & Thurs *order sheets

Chapter Three – Debunking Myths

*Write 30min 3 X week

*Sort & chop #1

Kim exercise M-W-F

Dan Thurs.

brkfst & shopping

*Interact X2/week

Summary

It is often thought that if the brain goes through severe trauma or injury, it would be difficult for it to recover fully. But our brains are more resilient than we think and they have the remarkable ability to recover from trauma. There are many other brain-related myths that people have, particularly concerning aging brains.

In this chapter we debunk some of these age-related brain myths and look at how you can help "de-age" your brain, thereby adding more years to its health.

Dr. Gupta shares a story about how he operated on a soldier under challenging circumstances in the Iraqi desert. Despite suffering massive injury to his brain, the soldier came through the whole experience completely healed. This shows us how resilient our brains can be. If our brains can recover from trauma, it is likely we can add more years to its health and de-age it.

12 Myths about the aging brain

1. The brain is a mystery – researchers and neuroscientists have made great strides into how our inner black box ticks. We now know more about the different connections in the brain and can identify which areas are responsible for addiction, depression and, obsessive-compulsive disorder (OCD). Neuroscience is constantly making new and exciting discoveries about the brain as more research and studies are carried out.

2. As you get older you are doomed to get more forgetful – a tiny part of this may hold some truth because some cognitive skills do decline as you get older. However, you can use strategies to help you remember better. Also, while you may not be as quick as a younger person in learning a new language for instance, other functions improve with age such as a superior vocabulary and the ability to better control your emotions.

3. Dementia will inevitably set in as you age – not true at all, dementia is not a normal part of old age. It can be avoided.

4. Older adults are not able to learn new things – here again, this is not true because learning never needs to stop. Memory is dynamic and we can grow new neurons which means we also have the capacity to learn new things or new skills.

5. Before you start learning another language, you must master the first – children who learn more than one language at a time are able to do so without confusing the two.

6. Memory training ensures you never forget – as with any other kind of training it has to be maintained. Ongoing practice maintains the strength of any muscle.

7. We use only 10 percent of our brains – one of the more well-known myths about our brains. Experiments and scans show that this is simply not true because much of the brain is used even when we are engaged in simple tasks. It may be true that we don't use all of our brain all of the time but all parts are necessary and we need all the different connections.

8. Intelligence and learning abilities are different between male and female brains – while there are some differences, it is not enough to say that one is better "equipped" than the other. Scientists are still busy studying these differences. It has been noted however that more women in the US have Alzheimer's than men. It is not clear as yet why women are at higher risk. A possibility could be that early symptoms are not picked up in women. Since women have more highly developed verbal skills than men it is easier to hide the symptoms.

9. Doing daily crossword puzzles helps prevent cognitive decline – crossword puzzles only challenge a portion of your brain – the word-finding ability known as fluency. Engaging in word and number puzzles though does have advantages. They

may not keep your brain sharp in general but they do help with memory, reasoning, and attention in some people.

10. We are either left-brain or right-brain dominant – another common misbelief. Brain scans show that the two hemispheres of the brain work together. The brain uses both the left and right sides for language processing, reading, and math.

11. We have five senses – in addition to the five senses that everyone is familiar with i.e., sight, smell, taste, touch, and hearing the brain also processes six other senses. These are a sense of balance, a sense of pain, a sense of where your body parts are and what they are doing, a sense of temperature, a sense of the passage of time, and a sense of our internal needs like hunger or thirst.

12. You are born with a certain number of brain cells and that's it – as we move from baby stages to childhood and later, our brains continue to grow and develop. The brain only reaches its maximum size in our tweens (for girls) and teens (for boys). As adults, the number of neurons (nerve cells) grows larger. And throughout life, the brain can rewire itself as you experience new things and prune away parts that are not being used.

The Five Pillars of brain health

Depending on the lifestyle choices we make, we can have a huge impact on our brain's ability to age well, stay healthy and keep sharp. Dr. Gupta refers to "superagers", people who are able to maintain a youthful brain well into old age. These people have memories as sharp as people much younger than them and their brains show no signs of age-related shrinkage. According to scientists, this may not be due to genetics only but to how you live your life.

In part 2 of his book, Dr. Gupta suggests applying the "five pillars of brain health" to our lives to help keep our brains sharp. The five pillars arise out of actions that are necessary for promoting good cognitive function across one's lifespan. They are move, discover, relax, nourish and connect.

Move, as you would expect is about exercise. Aerobic and nonaerobic (strength training) exercises are good for both the body and the brain. Physical exertion exercises the body and stimulates one's mind, improving brain health and functions. Movement keeps you more alert all through the day resulting in increased productivity.

Discover, is about learning new things like finding a new hobby or learning a new language. This helps to strengthen the brain and allows you to discover your brain's full capacity.

Relax so that your brain can chill out too, not just your body. Ensuring you have a good quality sleep can be good for brain health.

Nourish refers to the link between your diet and brain health. Evidence shows that consuming certain foods can help with memory loss and cognitive decline.

Connect with others either in person or even through social media. Social connections and interactions can improve our brain's plasticity. They also help to preserve our cognitive abilities.

We will expand on how you can incorporate these five pillars for optimal brain health into your daily life with more details in part two of this workbook.

Key Insights from this Chapter

1. There are many common myths about the aging brain that prove to be false.

2. Our brains are more resilient than we think.

3. Physical movement has been scientifically documented to help in improving brain health and brain function.

4. The five pillars of brain health can help you keep a sharp mind.

Identify Related Issues

1. Have you experienced brain injury or brain trauma in the past?

2. Which of the 12 myths did you believe were true before today?

3. I would like to believe that my brain health can be improved.

Goals You Want to Achieve

1. 5 Pillars.

   I would like to adhere to the five pillars of brain health which are to:

   M _____

   D _____

   R _____

   N _____

   C _____

   Can you fill them in?
   Think of also 1 activity which you can do that is connected to each pillar.

Your Plan of Action

1. Learn more about any of the myths that are related to symptoms I can relate to.

2. Share with others this new information I have learned about brain myths.

3. Move on to part two of this book, so I can learn how to incorporate the five pillars into my lifestyle.

Action Checklist

1. Test your knowledge of what you have learned about the brain so far. Tick the appropriate box.

Brain Facts	True	False
The human brain once damaged cannot be healed		✓
As we age our cognitive functions inevitably decline		✓
Our brains are more resilient than we think	✓	
All memory lapses are a sign of cognitive decline		✓
The left brain and the right brain often work together to process many functions	✓	
Doing daily crossword puzzles are enough to prevent cognitive decline		✓
Our brain cells stop growing when we reach adulthood		✓
Physical movement helps maintain brain health	✓	
What we eat has an effect on our brains	✓	
It is possible to keep our brains sharp as we get older	✓	

Answers can be found at the end of the book.

Part Two – Maintaining a Healthy Brain

Chapter Four – Why Movement is Important

Summary

One of the best ways to enhance your brain's function and improve its resiliency is by moving more. Exercise has been proven to trigger biological effects that help the brain stay sharp and healthy. Just like your body needs exercise to stay healthy so does your brain.

Scientists are beginning to notice that people who engage in sports that are 35 years and older benefit from exercise both physically and mentally. They also found that one of the risk factors in cognitive decline is physical inactivity.

The importance of regular exercise

Engaging in regular exercise – at least 150 minutes a week – is beneficial to brain health. Incorporating interval and strength training into your routine is important. Strength training where you use weights or your own body weight as resistance not only helps to tone and build muscle mass but also helps with balance and coordination.

The most common reason many people don't incorporate exercise into their daily schedules is because they say "I don't' have time". However, Dr. Gupta says you have to make time. Did you know that illnesses like high blood pressure and diabetes can increase your chance of suffering from dementia? Well, exercise has been found to be a powerful tool that helps you gain control of these types of illnesses.

Not only does exercise have physical healing powers but it also helps to make you mentally sharper. Yes, exercise helps you lose weight, it improves your metabolism and digestion while at the same time toning your body. It can also, according to Dr. Gupta "turn on your 'smart genes', support emotional stability, and stave off depression and dementia." In addition, exercise plays a role in boosting your self-worth and confidence.

How does physical exercise help the brain?

Exercise gives your brain a boost to help you think more clearly and to be more focused. Have you ever noticed after you have exercised, even after a short brisk walk, that you feel more energetic and mentally alert? Try it and see.

Studies are emerging that show the brain atrophying (degenerating) or actually physically shrinking from sedentarism (couch potato syndrome). Prolonged sitting with no physical activity can lead to an early death. When you sit for hours and hours at a time, your blood circulation slows down and your body uses less of your blood sugar. This means that more sugar is circulating in your blood (not good!).

Sitting slows down your metabolic rate and you stop burning as many calories. It also puts your muscles in a more dormant state which can lead to muscle atrophy. Activity even for a few minutes can counter these negative effects of sitting for too long.

Throughout the ages, human beings have been in motion. It would have taken massive amounts of physical effort to find sources of food and water back in the age of early civilization. So as Dr. Gupta puts it our genome (genetic instructions) "expects and requires frequent movement". In other words, we are supposed to move, we were not designed to sit or lie down for hours and hours.

The medical community recognizes that there is a strong link between movement of our bodies and our brain health. Studies have shown exercise benefits not only the body but also helps to reduce senility. Dr. Gupta lists several ways in which exercise is linked to positive brain health:

- Controlling your blood sugar through exercise means you will use sugar to fuel your muscles thereby preventing glucose and insulin fluctuations which increase the risk for dementia

- Exercise helps lower inflammation which is important in preventing dementia
- Your overall energy, stamina, strength, and flexibility will increase
- Blood and lymph circulation as well as oxygen supply to your cells and tissues increase
- Exercise helps to reduce stress and helps you have a better quality sleep; it releases endorphins (brain chemicals that are natural mood lifters and pain relievers)
- It helps to maintain your weight and helps you to build a stronger immune system
- Improves heart health, reducing the risk for cardiovascular disease and high blood pressure
- Exercise facilitates oxygenated blood flow, helping to deliver nutrients essential for cell growth and maintenance to the brain.

Through his travels and experience, Dr. Gupta has observed that leading a physically active life does indeed help one to have a sharper mind. Physically active people have a lower risk of cognitive decline and maintain better processing skills in aging brains. He has found that for him, exercise helps him think better and helps with consolidating new information.

The benefits of physical exercise for:

Stressed people

When you are stressed, your body releases a stress-related hormone called cortisol. Cortisol has been linked to long-lasting brain changes. Young people who are exposed to chronic stress early in life are often prone to anxiety and mood disorders as they grow.

Chronic stress together with higher levels of cortisol has been found to affect memory and learning negatively. Too much cortisol leads to an underproduction of neurons which in turn leads to the shrinking of the hippocampus (our brain's memory hub). Exercise helps you to better control stress and the flood of cortisol that results from it.

Older people

Dr Gupta says it is a myth that exercise is dangerous as you get older because the body gets frail. He says there is no reason why exercise cannot be a lifetime activity. It will "boost your brain in ways that can physically de-age you while preventing and even treating frailty". Exercise is one of the best ways to increase mobility in older people.

People with high blood sugar

The rate of cognitive decline in people with high blood sugar levels is faster than in those who have normal blood sugar. High blood sugar weakens your blood vessels increasing your chances of experiencing ministrokes in the brain. Ministrokes in the brain can trigger various forms of dementia. Another factor to consider is that when you take in too much simple sugars it makes cells, including brain cells, insulin resistant. This means that although insulin is present it cannot work well so brain cells cannot properly absorb sugar which is needed to fuel their activity.

The importance of white matter

White matter is found in the deeper tissues of the brain. It contains nerve fibers, which are extensions of nerve cells. Healthy white matter means stronger connections between the areas of the brain.

Studies have shown that people who have a lower level of aerobic fitness and mild cognitive impairment have weaker white matter. These people when tested did not do so well on memory and reasoning tests. Therefore, one can conclude that being physically fit encourages healthier white matter which is linked to better memory and reasoning abilities.

It is never too late to begin a physical exercise routine.

Have you noticed that as you get older your energy levels and muscle mass reduce? It is important to not only make exercise a part of your daily routine but to also add more variety to your fitness regime. Try to combine aerobic cardio work such as swimming, cycling, jogging, or group exercise classes with strength training (gym machines, free weights, squats, etc.) with routines that promote balance and flexibility such as yoga and stretching exercises.

Throughout the day try to be more physical with whatever you do such as taking the stairs instead of the elevator and avoiding prolonged sitting. Regular exercise (at least for about 150 minutes per week) even if it is as moderate as walking has been shown to have great benefits for brain health. If you don't already have a regular workout, start now and gradually increase the intensity of your workouts. Also, don't forget to vary them and do not be afraid to try new things.

Key Insights from this Chapter

1. A healthy brain comes with a healthy body.

2. Movement helps you to increase, repair, and maintain brain cells.

3. Exercise boosts blood flow to your brain, promotes growth of new cells, and lowers inflammation.

4. Regular physical exercise can help to limit the effects of cognitive decline.

5. You need at least 150 mins of exercise a week.

Identify Related Issues

1. Do you suffer from high blood pressure, diabetes, cardiovascular disease or obesity?

2. Do you sit for many hours without movement in your day?

3. Do you think you need to include more movement in your day?

4. Do you have a regular exercise routine?

5. If you do not currently have an exercise routine, do you think you should start one?

Goals You Want to Achieve

1. Move more. Increase my physical exercise.

2. Make sure I do not sit for long periods

3. Incorporate something new into my exercise routine.

4. Start now and work up to at least 150 minutes a week in the next 3 months.

5. Incorporate interval and strength training into my workout routine

Your Plan of Action

1. Make exercise a priority. Start with 5–10 minutes working up to 20 mins at least 3 times a week.

2. Incorporate strength training (weightlifting) and aerobic exercises into my exercise routine.

3. Get up and move away from my desk periodically to take a 2-minute walk or a quick stretch

Action Checklist

1. I am doing as much as I can to incorporate more physical movement/exercise into my day. For instance, I

   - Take the stairs instead of the elevator.

   - Replace sitting with walking or standing. If you can have a work conversation on the phone while you walk or stand, do it, it is better than sitting.

   - If you are already exercising regularly try something different. If you are a jogger, try cycling or swimming.

2. If you do an activity not on this list, add it here:

   - _____

   - _____

Activities To Do to boost physical movement

- _____

- _____

- _____

- _____

Chapter Five – Keep The Brain Active

Summary

Did you know that people who retire early can be at risk of developing dementia? The longer you stay working the more you tend to be socially connected, physically active, and mentally challenged. This is not to say you have to work forever, but if you are able to, delay retirement for as long as you can.

When you do retire, you should continue to engage in activities that will keep you socially connected and stimulated. Maintaining a sense of purpose gives your life meaning and direction. When you continue to learn and discover new things, your life takes on a sense of purpose and this is active aging.

In chapter 4 we spoke about keeping your body active with exercise and how this can lead to a healthy brain. **Active aging** involves more than just getting your body to move, it also involves getting your brain to move. When you use your brain in challenging ways it improves your overall brain heath.

When you challenge your brain in the "right way, it helps you to tap into its 'plastic' power, that is the brain's ability to rewire itself". It is quite possible for a person whose brain shows signs of Alzheimer's disease at an autopsy to have lived a normal life without any cognitive decline. How is this possible? Scientists call this ability brain resiliency or the cognitive reserve that the brain has.

To build brain resiliency which can possibly protect against cognitive decline, one has to stay engaged as much as possible. Socializing as well as being actively involved in stimulating activities helps with this. In chapter 8 we will look at why it is so important to maintain your connection to other people. In this chapter, we focus on cognitive reserve.

What is cognitive reserve?

It is a backup system in the brain, but no one is sure how it works exactly. This is how Dr. Gupta defines it:

Cognitive reserve is your brain's ability to improvise and navigate

around impediments it may encounter that could prevent it from getting a job done.

Your brain's cognitive reserve develops over time, usually through learning, discovery, education, and natural curiosity. According to some researchers, a "robust" cognitive reserve can help you function well through life events like chronic stress or environmental toxins for instance, which require extra effort from the brain.

Building and maintaining your cognitive reserve can be done by involving your brain in demanding activities that keep it thinking and learning. When you continuously challenge your brain to do things like strategize or solve problems or learn new things, you are ultimately building new networks in your brain and strengthening the existing ones.

We have mentioned earlier that the brain has plastic power, i.e., new brain cell growth which can happen throughout your lifetime. This means that you can work to stimulate your brain and improve cognitive development at any age despite your previous education levels.

Brain stimulating activities

Gaming

Different activities for stimulating your brain have been around for a while. Some, such as games, puzzles, and brain-training videos can help to improve your working memory but they are not great for brain functions such as reasoning and problem-solving. They are not challenging enough.

It has been found that learning another language and speed training video games can be effective at slowing down age-related decline. Certain types of video games can be useful to train our brains to be better, faster, and stronger if they are designed specifically to improve brain health and function. Games that are designed to address a specific cognitive deficit can be more effective.

Living life with purpose

There is much to be said about how having a sense of purpose in your life can help you live longer and healthier. Studies show that older people who have a sense of purpose in life are less likely to develop ailments such as Alzheimer's disease, strokes, heart attacks, and cognitive impairment.

When you have purpose, you are motivated to take better care of yourself. When you have a sense of purpose, you become more optimistic which has a positive impact on mental well-being. To stay engaged and maintain your sense of purpose try doing things that get you into the "flow".

When you are in flow (in the groove, on fire) you are in a state of being totally immersed in an activity. You become deeply focused with no distractions. You have a feeling of intense energy which is more relaxed, not stressed and you feel challenged. Being immersed in a state of flow leaves you feeling stimulated, but to truly be in flow you must have a clear sense of purpose.

Key Insights from this Chapter

1. Keeping your brain active can help to protect it against cognitive decline.

2. Learning something new helps to strengthen brain cells.

3. Engage in cognitively stimulating activities that keep your brain thinking, learning, and strategizing.

4. Having a purpose in life can help you to keep your brain active.

Identify Related Issues

1. Do I ensure my brain is constantly being challenged?

2. Am I learning and discovering new things?

3. Do I have a sense of purpose?

Goals You Want to Achieve

1. I want to keep my brain active and have a clear sense of purpose.

2. I want to be able partake in **active aging** and exercise my brain as I do my body.

Your Plan of Action

1. Learn/discover/explore something new.

2. Totally immerse myself in an activity (get into a state of flow).

3. Define my purpose. This can be anything. It is however important that you identify strongly with it as a sense of purpose gives you the energy to overcome obstacles and centers you when the rest of the world might be in chaos. For example, if your find that your purpose in life is to be a monk or ascetic, then even whilst you aren't currently able to achieve that goal as yet, the very idea of it will still drive you forward and fuel you with resolve.

Action Checklist

1. Try something new. Crossword puzzles are good, but they only target a very specific area of the brain. Try firing up your neurons with something completely new. Learn a new skill or start a new hobby that completely immerses you. Move out of your comfort zone. Learn to play chess or a musical instrument or learn a new language or find a new hobby. Sign up for an online class. Many free classes are available on a wide range of topics by top-rated learning centers.

2. Try your hand at writing – writing improves communication abilities and working memory. It does not matter what you write, have fun and let your brain enjoy a workout at the same time. You can write in a diary or journal or write some poetry, stories, letters, emails, or even blog posts. Get creative.

3. Write down what you think your purpose is. Why do you do what you do? What keeps you going?

My Purpose In Life Is

_____

_____

_____

Chapter Six – Sleep and Relaxation

Summary

Many of us are chronically sleep-deprived which puts us at a higher risk for ailments such as dementia, learning and memory problems, mood disorders, depression, diabetes, weight gain and obesity, cancer, and fall-related injuries. Sleep deprivation can also affect our decision-making.

We need on average 7 to 8 hours of sleep a night to effectively reset our brains and bodies. When we sleep, we are not in a state of neural idleness; our brains and bodies are still active. During sleep our body replenishes itself. Therefore, it is important that we not only get an <u>adequate</u> amount of ZZZs but also <u>good quality</u> sleep. It is a myth that the body can catch up on missed sleep later on.

Advantages of good sleep

Studies have shown that our sleeping habits have an impact on everything we do. Your alertness is reduced by about a third when you get six or fewer hours of sleep a night. A brain that gets enough sleep is a well-rested and healthy brain.

Sleep disorders like sleep apnea which affects millions of people can be treated with lifestyle changes, to improve the quality of our sleep.

Sleep apnea refers to the ailment whereby the airway collapses during sleep because the muscles in the back of the throat are unable to keep the airway open. This results in fragmented sleep because breathing frequently ceases. A common condition resulting from sleep apnea is snoring.

Not getting enough sleep and sleep apnea often leads to a lack of energy and daytime exhaustion. This can increase the risk of developing heart disease and stroke.

Research shows that when we are asleep, significant events are encoded in our brain's memory banks. While we sleep our brains are actively filing away our most recent memories for later recall. This memory organizing that our brain does cannot take place without sleep.

Without sufficient sleep, it becomes harder to process information quickly and be as mentally alert as you can be. When you get enough sleep, you will be sharper, more creative, and more attentive.

A study conducted found that older adults who did not get enough sleep or had fragmented sleep are more at risk of developing Alzheimer's disease. It was also found that people who did get a good night's sleep were less prone to cognitive decline.

Another advantage of getting adequate and quality sleep is that while you are asleep your brain takes the opportunity to self-clean and get rid of brain waste. During sleep sticky proteins that can help form amyloid plaques are cleared or washed out. Amyloid plaques are litter that eventually causes inflammation and a buildup of tau proteins which can destroy neurons. If you do not get the chance to remove this "brain trash" you may have a higher risk of developing dementia and Alzheimer's disease. Sleep declutters the brain.

Dr. Gupta says that it is a myth that taking sleep aids will help you sleep better. He says that they will help you fall asleep faster but the quality of sleep you get will not be as restful as natural sleep. Some sleep aids such as Valium and Xanax are habit-forming and have been shown to be associated with developing dementia.

It is a vicious cycle. Once you get Alzheimer's then your sleep gets disrupted which worsens the damage.

Dr Gupta's secrets to getting good sleep

- Stick to a schedule; get up at the same time every day to establish a healthy circadian rhythm (your body's internal 24hr clock)
- Avoid long naps; they disrupt nighttime sleep
- Go to bed when you feel most sleepy before midnight
- Set your body clock in the morning by exposing your eyes to sunlight as soon as you wake up

- Regular exercise promotes good sleep
- Don't eat or drink for 3 hours before your bedtime
- Be aware of your medications as some can affect sleep; for example, some contain caffeine
- Ensure that your sleeping environment is cool, quiet, and dark; minimize light sources especially those from electronic devices
- Keep pets out of the bedroom; their movements can disrupt your sleep
- Try to eliminate using electronics in bed; the blue wavelength from these devices have been known to suppress the hormone melatonin needed for sleep
- Establish bedtime rituals and make sure to disconnect from any stimulating tasks
- Instead engage in calming activities just before bedtime such as listening to soothing music or a warm bath.

If all these methods don't work, talk to your doctor or find a sleep study that you can undergo. Sleep labs monitor and record your sleep to find the underlying problems.

Relaxation

Daytime rest and relaxation are also important. While sleep rejuvenates us, we also need to find activities that allow us to relax for our mental well-being. Many people are finding that mindfulness practices, deep breathing, meditation, and yoga are very beneficial for relaxation. These types of activities also lower the levels of cortisol (stress hormone).

Dr. Gupta suggests some other R and R strategies that can help you build a more resilient brain. They include:

- Volunteering – people who volunteer have less anxiety and loneliness
- Express gratitude – lowers stress and increases empathy
- Practice forgiveness – promotes life satisfaction and makes you feel better about yourself
- Find laughter triggers – look for what makes you laugh; when you laugh the feel-good hormone serotonin is triggered. Laughter reduces stress and tension.
- Take a break from social media – schedule a time for checking notifications and emails and stick to that time only
- Create or find an extra hour in your day – if you cut down on screen time you can most likely find that extra hour that you can use to exercise or meditate
- Reward yourself – for instance, practice rewarding yourself such as giving yourself a 5-minute break after 25 minutes of working on a task
- Do not multitask – the brain does not like multi-tasking. Tasks that require conscious effort, thinking, comprehension or skill require focused concentration. Do one at a time and avoid distractions. Multi-tasking slows down your thinking.
- Plan and prioritize – identify your priorities for the day and plan accordingly

- Manage your environment – declutter; throw out what you no longer need. Mess and clutter create stress and can be distracting.
- Set aside at least 15 minutes each day for yourself – use this time to engage in some type of destressing activity. Sit quietly and focus on your breathing or write in a journal. When you focus on your breath, pay attention to it going in and coming out of your nose. When it goes in, note that the breath is going in. When it goes out, note that it is going out. Most folks tend to establish a focal point at the space between the tip of the nose and the upper lip. This is where the breath can be felt traversing in and out. While focusing on the breath, should you have any wandering thoughts, steer your mind back to the breath. Do not give prolonged attention to the thoughts. Your primary focus should always be the breath.
- Daydream – allow yourself to daydream; it acts as a neural rest button.

Life transitions are natural to everyone; we all go through phases in our lives that bring different challenges. From the birth of children to retirement we learn to adapt through our changing circumstances. Midlife – between the ages of thirty-five and fifty-five is the period when our stressors tend to peak. Many people suffer from depression during this period of their lives which is a risk factor for dementia. To keep sharp and mentally well, keep track of your stress and try to get adequate sleep and relaxation to reduce stress.

Key Insights from this Chapter

1. Poor sleep can lead to impaired memory while good sleep keeps us sharp and attentive.

2. We need restorative sleep every night. Sleep helps us to consolidate learning and experiences.

3. Chronic stress, anxiety, and depression can increase dementia risks whereas rest and relaxation help to reduce the risk

Identify Related Issues

1. Do you get enough undisturbed sleep every night?

2. Are you a night owl, who takes naps during the day?

3. Do you have a bedtime ritual that allows you to relax?

4. Do you take your electronic devices to bed with you at night?

5. Do you get any rest or relaxation during the day?

Goals You Want to Achieve

1. Ensure I get a good night's sleep every night/Improve my sleeping habits.

2. Try to find a few minutes to rest/relax during the day.

3. Take breaks from social media and cut down on multi-tasking

Your Plan of Action

1. Establish a bedtime routine and ensure I keep to the same times.

2. Find an activity I like that I know will help me relax/destress and try to fit it into my daily routine.

3. Analyze the amount of time I distract myself with social media and make an effort to cut down on this time.

Action Checklist

1. Pick one of these stress-reducing activities to engage in or anything else not on this list that appeals to you.
   a. dance
   b. take a relaxing bath
   c. listen to chill music
   d. knitting (the repetitive action can be quite calming),
   e. do some stretching exercise or enroll for a yoga class

f. meditate or practice conscious breathing
g. doodle (adult coloring books)
h. read or listen to a podcast
i. express gratitude
j. forgive others
k. breathe deeply
l. laugh more
m. declutter – mess creates stress

2. Write down what type of sleep/relaxation routine you think would work for you and try it out over the next few weeks. You may need to experiment a bit and make changes until you find what works best for you.

_____

_____

_____

_____

_____

_____

3. After 12 weeks, come back to this chapter and answer the following questions?
    a. Have you made a plan to ensure you get enough sleep every night?
    b. Are you getting the restorative sleep you require to give your brain a chance to repair, grow and rest?
    c. Have you noticed any improvement in your levels of tiredness and mental alertness after you have had proper sleep?

Chapter Seven – Eating for Brain Health

Summary

Every day we are inundated with information about what to eat and what to avoid. Sometimes the information we get is contradictory. One day we are told that coffee is bad for you, the next, it's good for you or this is a superfood and that has too much sugar and so on. You are urged to follow a specific diet; today it's low carbs, paleo, or keto, next month it's gluten-free or lactose-free or low cholesterol, low fat, vegan, or Mediterranean.

How do you decide which one to follow? Do you just pick the one you think might work for you and if it doesn't, move on to the next? Or do you talk to your doctor about it? Gupta says that most doctors seldom discuss nutritional needs with their patients. In this chapter, we look at what is the best diet for your brain.

Brain health and diet

Evidence shows that the diet you feed your body is connected to your brain health. Your dietary style (your way of eating) makes a big difference to your short-term and long-term health. When choosing what is best for you there are many different factors to take into account. Ultimately though this will narrow down to your preferences and what suits your lifestyle. Whatever nutritional plan you follow, in this chapter we focus on what will help you foster brain health.

In his book, Dr. Gupta talks about a couple of diets that had some good results for brain health such as the Mediterranean diet and the MIND diet. You might want to look them up if you want to learn more about them. They do seem to work better than most others in reducing the risk for dementia and Alzheimer's. Studies conducted show that people on a Mediterranean-style diet for instance "enjoy greater brain volume as they age."

Have you heard of "superfoods"? You will have noticed that the media and advertisers are always promoting certain foods as superfoods for the brain. Dr. Gupta says that while these superfoods may indeed have good health benefits, this does not mean they are superior in any way to other foods that provide good health benefits. Although foods like fresh blueberries and omega-3-rich nuts/seeds are "supergood" for you they do not necessarily target the brain as claimed.

It has often been said that a heart-healthy diet is also good for brain health. Many studies have shown that indeed heart health and brain health do have many connections. Dr. Richard Isaacson, a neurologist from Cornell University conducted research which led him to believe that to prevent and treat dementia one needs to have a personalized nutrition plan since no single patient is the same. We need to take into account a person's genes, environment, and lifestyle.

No single food or superfood targets brain health specifically, but Dr. Gupta believes that with the right combination of foods we can secure our brain health now and in the future. Typical Western diets that are high in salt, sugar and saturated fats are not brain-friendly.

One should also not rely on vitamins and supplements to do the job for you. They are beneficial, but only when taken as part of a balanced diet so they can be properly absorbed in order to work. A plant-based diet that is rich in fresh vegetables and fruit, particularly leafy green veggies and berries is better for brain health.

Sanjay Gupta's Guide to eating for brain health

Changing to a diet that optimizes your brain will not happen overnight. You can start by making small shifts like including more leafy green veggies or fruit into your current eating plan. The best thing is to find out what works for you and make it a part of your routine. In Chapter 9 of his book, Dr. Gupta offers food plan ideas for you to build an individualized plan for yourself. He says a simple way to start now is to aim to include seven different colored foods.

For himself, he spent a few years focusing on creating an eating plan that he can maintain easily, even when he is traveling.

This takes planning and commitment and of course, you need to also take into account your family and your budget. This may take some time, but what you should do right now to start you on the right track is to reduce the foods that are bad for your brain immediately, such as salty foods, sugar, and processed foods.

In his guide to good eating, he uses his **SHARP** acronym to explain what you should eat for good brain health:

S – Slash the sugar and stick to your ABCs

We all know that too much sugar is bad for you, but do you know it is toxic for your body and a high-sugar diet affects your brain health? This is because people with a high blood sugar level have been shown to have a faster rate of cognitive decline than those with a normal blood sugar level. Cutting back on the amount of sugar you consume slashes your risk for blood sugar imbalances, insulin resistance, and dementia.

ABCs refer to foods that are considered to be on the A-list of foods to consume regularly. B-list foods are ones you can include in your diet and C-list foods are the ones you should limit. These foods are known to be good or bad for brain health. Examples of the top-quality ones from the A-list are fresh vegetables (especially leafy greens such as spinach and kale), whole berries, fish and seafood, nuts and seeds, and healthy fats such as extra virgin olive oil, avocados, and whole eggs.

Foods on the B-list include legumes (beans, lentils, etc.), whole fruits, whole grains, poultry, and low sugar, low-fat dairy such as cottage cheese or plain yogurt.

Foods we should try to avoid or limit fall into the C-list. These include fried foods, pastries, sugary foods, and processed foods. Try to cut down on salt, red meat products like bacon, dairy that is high in saturated fats such as cheese and butter, and red meat (beef, lamb, pork, duck, etc.)

H – Hydrate smartly

Sometimes it is difficult to realize when we are thirsty and this can result in dehydration. As we get older our ability to perceive thirst becomes harder. Another problem is that often we mistake thirst for hunger. To counter these two factors, you should drink before you feel thirsty or drink first before you reach for a snack, to check if you were thirsty instead of hungry.

Dehydration is not good for the body or the brain. It saps your energy and can lead to cognitive problems in older people. According to researchers, even moderate dehydration in older people can lead to confusion and disorientation. The more dehydrated you are the more your thinking skills will be affected.

Some studies have shown that drinking tea or coffee is associated with a decrease in the risk of cognitive decline and dementia. Studies show that coffee is good for mental alertness and cognitive performance. If you are a caffeine consumer, make sure you do not let it disturb your sleep.

Whatever you opt for whether it's water, tea or coffee the important lesson is to stay hydrated.

A – Add more omega-3 fatty acids from dietary sources

Omega-3 fatty acids found in brain-nourishing foods such as seafood and nuts and seeds are very good for brain health. However, Omega-6 fats, found in corn and vegetable oils often used in fried, baked, and processed foods are bad for you. Unfortunately, as Americans, we consume too much Omega-6 and too little Omega-3.

Try to cut down on Omega-6 foods and include more Omega-3 rich foods in your diet. Good sources are fatty fish (salmon and sardines), flaxseed, chia seeds, pumpkin seeds, sunflower seeds, and plant-derived oils (olive, canola, etc.).

Remember food sources are always better than supplements. Research has found that eating fish or seafood more often (instead of taking fish oil tablets) contributes to better brain health than people who don't consume fish and seafood often. Eating right can make the taking of supplements unnecessary.

R – Reduce portions

This is a no-brainer – portion control – we all know we should not go back for seconds! But when it's family feast time, it's hard to control oneself. Over-indulging occasionally is okay but try to watch your portions on a daily basis. Preparing meals at home (instead of takeaways or eating out) helps to control your portions and caloric intake.

How you cook your food also makes a big difference. Boiling, steaming, poaching or baking is always better than fried. So, in addition to controlling your portion and your calories, also try to control your cooking methods. Avoid unnecessary oils and sauces as much as you can.

Some people have found that intermittent fasting has helped them to control when they eat and the number of calories they consume. When fasting is done correctly it can increase BDNF, a protein that helps to strengthen and protect neural connections in the brain. This protein also helps to spur the growth of new brain cells. If you decide to try fasting, speak to your doctor first.

P – Plan ahead

Are you one of those people who suddenly realize you are hungry or you haven't eaten lunch yet and you reach out for whatever is quick and convenient? When you do not plan your meals ahead of time you end up eating what is quick and tasty even if it is not healthy. Try to plan your main meals in advance and keep healthy snacks on hand.

Here are some extra tips to keep in mind when planning your meals:

- Organic or grass-fed beef has less total fat and more omega-3 fatty acids
- Curcumin the main active ingredient in turmeric has great antioxidant, antifungal, and anti-inflammatory properties; it also seems to help with memory and attention
- Use smaller plates to control portion sizes
- Eat fish at least twice a week
- Eat a wide variety of different colored veggies
- Check the salt content of herbs and spices and other condiments
- Prepare meals at home

When doing your grocery shopping remember to include sources of fiber in your meals. Fiber is key to brain health; it has been shown to help prevent depression and dementia.

Key Insights from this Chapter

1. Consuming certain foods can help avoid memory and brain decline.

2. To maximize your brain's performance, follow the SHARP guide.

3. Hydration is very important for brain function. Dehydration (even slightly) affects your attention, memory, and other cognitive functions.

4. Plan your meals in advance to avoid take-outs and unhealthy snacking.

Identify Related Issues

1. Am I eating to nourish my brain?

2. Do have enough brain food in my diet?

3. Are my portion sizes too large?

4. Do I plan my meals in advance?

5. Do I hydrate enough, do I eat too much sugar or junk food?

Goals You Want to Achieve

1. Aim for clean living and clean eating

2. Improve the way I eat and what I eat

3. Plan meals ahead

4. Cut down on sugar and fast foods and increase my omega-3 intake

5. Make sure I hydrate enough

Your Plan of Action

1. Prepare more home-cooked meals and plan meals ahead to avoid reliance on fast food

2. Watch my calorie intake and reduce my portions

3. Incorporate more brain-healthy foods such as fish into my meals

4. Increase my intake of hydrating liquids.

5. Cut down on supplements and focus more on incorporating the real foods that are rich vitamins and minerals into my meals.

Action Checklist

1. Use the SHARP system to change up my diet

2. Make a plan to eat smart

3. Rethink how I shop for food:

4. Add more brain-beneficial foods such as extra virgin olive oil, nuts, seeds, berries, whole fruits, leafy greens, and cold-water fish to my shopping list. Limit foods that are high in sugar, salt, saturated fats, and trans fats like butter and cheese.

Chapter Eight - The People Connection

Summary

Connecting with others, continual social interactions, and having a social network are important factors in protecting your brain against cognitive decline. We know that meaningful relationships and their accompanying interactions bring us love, happiness, comfort, and an escape from loneliness. But, did you know that relationships also influence our other health functions such as brain health, cardiovascular health, and endocrine and immune systems?

Social connections

As human beings we need social connections to thrive; we crave interactions with others. Socialization has positive impacts on our overall health as well as our brain health. It helps keep our minds strong and our memories intact. But this does not mean that if you have hundreds of social connections, it is enough. To thrive, you have to have some quality relationships.

Researchers found that married couples are less likely to experience cognitive decline or dementia as they age.

Companionship and regular meaningful interactions seem to help in protecting us from the effects of stress on our brains. Social isolation and the absence of real connections can have awful mental, physical and emotional consequences. This is especially so for older adults who live alone.

It has been found that people with fewer social connections have:

- Disrupted sleep patterns
- More inflammation
- Higher levels of stress hormones
- Altered immune systems

And they are lonely. Loneliness has been shown to speed up cognitive decline. It is therefore important for us to nurture the relationships we have as much as we take care of our health.

A study called the Synapse Project found that older adults who participated in challenging activities showed improvement in cognitive and brain functions. When you engage with a social group and participate in some kind of challenging activity with the group you are more likely to be protected against Alzheimer's disease.

Social isolation has many damaging effects. Children who are socially isolated often have poorer health. Adults who are isolated feel lonely to such an extent that it leads to feelings of melancholy and actual physical pain.

Close relationships contribute to our happiness and contentment and can help delay mental and physical decline.

Dr. Gupta suggests that one of the major ingredients to a long, sharp life is authentic connections with others. The quality of the connections you have matters. One study by Dr. Waldinger concluded that people who were in relationships where they could count on one another in times of need had memories that tended to stay sharper for a longer time. Those who were in relationships where they did not feel they could count on the other person experienced memory decline much earlier.

Social media connections

Older people that Dr. Gupta met who use the Internet to stay in touch with family and friends generally appeared happier. Having the Internet allowed them to learn and to connect with other people. This shows that digital engagement is not always as negative as what many tend to make it out to be. It can have positive effects, particularly on the cognitive abilities of older adults.

With so much of the world now relying more on digital media to communicate with one another, its role in maintaining connections is important especially for those that live in remote places. For others though, one should not replace in-person communication with social media. Face-to-face interactions are still valuable.

Stay socially engaged

It is important to ensure that you stay socially engaged. Connect regularly with friends and relatives. Maintain social connections with people of different ages. Try to have at least one trustworthy person you can confide in. We all need a confidante. One of the most beneficial things for your brain is to walk with a friend or neighbor. This gives you both a chance to walk (physical activity), connect and talk through anything that might be worrying you.

If you are looking to make new connections, try volunteering at a school or a local community center. Focus on maintaining the relationships you do have. Many people who live alone adopt a pet. Consider that if you need to. The benefits of interacting with animals range from reducing depression and anxiety to increased physical activity (walking your dog).

Good relationships give your brain a boost and a healthy brain boosts a good relationship in turn. It does not matter if your brain is not razor-sharp for you to have good relationships. Dr. Gupta makes the point that people who are living with dementia need to keep in touch with other people.

Key Insights from this Chapter

1. Maintaining your social connections can help you with keeping your brain active.

2. Having a social network helps to preserve your cognitive abilities, reduces stress, and boosts your immune system.

3. Loneliness/social isolation is an important cause of cognitive decline.

4. Find at least one person you can regularly confide in.

Identify Related Issues

1. Do I make enough effort to maintain my social connections?

2. Do I engage with diverse groups of people on a regular basis?

3. Who can I count on in times of need?

Goals You Want to Achieve

1. Ensure I regularly connect/keep in touch with my closest connections.

2. Try to widen the diversity of my connections/interact with diverse people.

3. Talk about my stressors with a close connection.

Your Plan of Action

1. Call friends and family regularly to catch up.

2. Interact with people of different age groups in my neighborhood, community centers, etc.

3. Go for walks with my close friend/someone I feel I can confide in.

Action Checklist

1. I am having regular video/phone chats with family and friends.

2. I am building social networks and participating in social activities like group exercise classes or clubs.

3. I go out for lunch or dinner dates with a family member or a friend.

Chapter Nine – 12 Weeks to A Sharper You

<u>Summary</u>

We have unique minds that are all our own and we should never take them for granted. Our minds are what shape our unique perceptions of the world around us and we must keep them as sharp as we can and for as long as we can.

In the preceding chapters, we looked at some of the strategies Dr. Gupta provides in his book, to keep your mind sharp. In this chapter we look at the 12-week program he put together to help you implement the Five Pillars.

Putting his strategies into practice may not be easy at first; change is never easy and breaking long-established habits is even harder. Dr. Gupta advises you to start the program and see how you feel after the first week or two. He says that you do not need to follow his program to the T but that you should do what you can. Make it your aim to establish at least one new habit a week if you can.

The 5 goals of the 12-week program are to:

MOVE MORE

STIMULATE YOUR BRAIN IN NEW WAYS

GET ENOUGH REST

NOURISH YOUR BODY APPROPRIATELY

CONNECT AND MAINTAIN AUTHENTIC CONNECTIONS

In the first week of the program, you are advised to start five new habits each day based on the five pillars and then you must repeat those habits in the second week. In the third week, you will include more habits into your days until you reach the final 12th week. For many people, it will take longer than 12 weeks to establish these new habits in their lives, but the first 12 weeks are to get you started.

Gupta's 12-week program to better brain health does not require you to purchase anything special. You will however need to do some planning (to schedule exercise and do menu planning for instance). If you find that you do not like one of the suggestions, you can either skip it or replace it with an alternative. The idea behind this program is for you to be able to tailor it to your own needs.

The Program

Weeks 1 and 2 – address five areas in your life to start building a better brain:

1. Move more

Try to incorporate more movement into your day. If you already have an exercise routine in place, change it up a bit. Do something that uses a new set of muscles, for example, if you are a runner, try cycling or swimming. Aim to work out a minimum of 30 minutes a day and incorporate strength training into your routine.

If you have not exercised in a long while, aim to ease yourself back into exercise slowly. Try to move at least twenty minutes three times a week. On days when your schedule is packed, try to incorporate physical activity with some of your daily tasks, for example taking the stairs at work instead of the elevator.

Limit the amount of time you spend sitting down. If you work at a desk the whole day, make a point to get up every 40mins or every hour for a 2–5-minute walk or even to stretch. Aim to do some type of physical activity every day. Your body and your brain will benefit.

2. Learn More

Explore how you can find new ways to stimulate your brain. Perhaps enrolling in a community adult education course, or reading about topics outside your normal field of interest?

3. Sleep Better

Establish a sleep routine. Start by ensuring you get at least 7 hours of sleep a night. Do not eat at least three hours before bedtime and try to go to bed and get up at the same time every day. Keep your bedroom electronics-free. See if you can include a stress-reducing strategy into your day, even for a few minutes.

4. Eat "Sanjay" style

According to Dr. Gupta, when you eat is as important as what you eat. He eats "breakfast like a king, lunch like a prince, and dinner like a peasant." Do you snack? Do you comfort-eat?

The first two weeks of the sharp program will help you to curb your cravings thereby reducing the need for snacking. During the first two weeks of the SHARP program, Dr. Gupta advises that you avoid eating out so you have less temptation.

Remember SHARP for brain health:

S – Less sugar

H – Hydrate more

A – Add omega-3

R – Reduce your portions

P – Plan your meals

Focus on eating a better, more nutritious breakfast. For instance, swap the bagel for oatmeal, skip the frappuccinos for black coffee. Instead of a processed lunch, pre-pack a salad or a healthy sandwich and replace energy drinks with water or tea. The same for dinner – try to avoid fast-food options.

5. Connect

This week make it a goal to reconnect with someone you have lost touch with or invite a friend over for dinner.

Weeks 3 and 4

In weeks 3 and 4, add more to the new routine you developed in the first two weeks. For example, go for a short power walk during your lunch break or try a bit of meditation to relax after work or before going to bed.

Weeks 5 and 6

Add more to your routine by choosing at least three of the following options:

- Start a gratitude journal
- Add a few more minutes to your exercise routine
- Avoid processed foods completely
- Try a yoga class or hiking
- Add some form of relaxing activity to your bedtime routine. Listening to soothing music might be a good suggestion.

Weeks 7 and 8

Once again, try to add more from Dr. Gupta's suggested list to your new routine:

- Look for volunteering opportunities in your community
- Find your local farmers market and buy fresh wholesome foods
- Schedule a doctor's visit for a checkup
- Write a letter/send a message sharing an important lesson you learned to a younger loved one
- If you enjoy reading, venture into new territory, try a different genre

Weeks 9 and 10

At this point, check if you are making the necessary changes and if they are working. Are you getting the right amount of sleep and exercise? Are you learning anything new or challenging? Are you following S.H.A.R.P.? Are you connecting?

Week 11

During this week Dr. Gupta encourages you to think about your wishes should you be diagnosed with dementia or Alzheimer's disease. How would you want your family members to deal with this? Write down your wishes.

Week 12

In the final week, make a list of all the changes you have made and the new habits you have started forming. Analyze what worked and what didn't work and why. See how you can adapt, make changes, or plan to meet your goals for the next 12 weeks.

Key Insights from this Chapter

1. With Dr. Gupta's personalized 12-week program you can strengthen your brain every day.

2. The 12-week program and pillars are useful for everyone, regardless of age.

Identify Related Issues

1. What obstacles are preventing me from starting Dr. Gupta's 12-week program?

2. Are there any areas of the program which are not fully clear to me?

Goals You Want to Achieve

1. I want to start the 12-week program.

2. I want to also maintain the program beyond the 12 weeks stipulated.

Your Plan of Action

1. Identify and make a plan to work around any obstacles to me starting the 12-week program.

2. Start the program as soon as I can.

3. Affirm to yourself that it is do-able and you have the ability to do it. Break any possible obstacles into micro tasks and clear these tasks on a daily or weekly basis. That way, even if you are not able to get started on the program right away, you maintain your effort and eagerness to start as you know you are working towards clearing any potential barriers

Action Checklist

1. Remind yourself:

    a. Check back on the goals you identified in chapters 4, 5, 6, 7 and 8

    b. What was your plan of action? Can you implement it now?

    c. Go through the action checklists for each of the chapters mentioned above to assist you to attain your goal here.

2. **YOU CAN DO IT!** Just start.

A journey of a thousand miles starts with one single step

Part Three – The Diagnosis and After

Chapter 10 – What to Do

Summary

In the final two chapters of his book, Dr. Gupta focuses on the challenges of being diagnosed with a brain disease, what it entails for you and your caregivers, and where to find help. A dementia diagnosis can have a devastating financial, physical and emotional toll on the family members of those who are diagnosed with it.

Everyone around the dementia patient, including the patient themselves suffer during the different stages of this disease – family, friends, caregivers, and volunteers. However, with early diagnosis, it is possible to minimize the devastating effects with planning, timely interventions, and coping strategies.

Since there is no cure yet for Alzheimer's, it is important to ensure you make healthy life choices that delay the onset or reduce the severity of the symptoms to reduce your risk for dementia. It is best not to ignore symptoms and seek medical help as soon as possible.

Since Alzheimer's disease can begin in the brain sometimes twenty to thirty years before the symptoms develop, this allows us to put into place lifestyle interventions that can delay or even prevent the disease from developing. These interventions include:

- Diet
- Exercise
- Sleep
- Supplements/drugs when necessary
- Intellectual stimulation
- Stress reduction strategies

Studies have shown that even a simple change in your diet can make a difference. Applying fundamental lifestyle habits to your life, as outlined in this workbook can delay the onset of dementia. The Keep Sharp plan which encourages a low-sugar, low-fat, whole foods, plant-based diet, moderate exercise, stress management, and maintaining social connections can help to nip the illness in the bud.

The Stages of Alzheimer's disease

Alzheimer's disease develops in three stages. These are mild (the early stage), moderate (the middle stage), and severe (the late stage). Everyone with the disease does not necessarily experience these 3 stages in the same way. Some move more quickly than others through the stages. For some the severity during a stage might be less, for others, it might be more.

A person with Alzheimer's can live four to eight years on average after being diagnosed, but depending on other factors they could live as long as twenty years.

Early Stage

At this stage, you still function independently and normally but you may notice some memory lapses and forget familiar words or the location of everyday items. Family members may also start noticing this. There may also be vision changes, an increasing inability to plan or solve problems, confusing time and place, finding difficulty in completing familiar tasks, misplacing things, and struggling a little to communicate.

Middle Stage

This is when you have moderate Alzheimer's and it is usually the longest stage which can last for many years. In this stage, the disease progresses and symptoms become more obvious and increase in severity.

Symptoms will include forgetting parts of one's own personal history, forgetting events, feeling moody, being confused about the days or where one is, changes in sleep patterns, wandering, getting lost, having trouble with bladder and bowel movements, behavioral changes like hand-wringing and personality changes. At this stage, depending on the severity of the symptoms you may need more care.

Late Stage

In this, the third stage of the disease noticeable personability changes occur and you lose your ability to carry on a conversation or control your movements. You will lose awareness of your surroundings, lose basic physical abilities, difficulty in communicating increases and you become more vulnerable to infections such as pneumonia. At this stage, you will need around-the-clock assistance.

Dementia Mimics

It is often very difficult to arrive at a diagnosis of Alzheimer's disease until the symptoms become severe. A diagnosis usually involves a team of specialists and different approaches and tools. Sometimes there are "dementia mimics" that can be misdiagnosed for Alzheimer's disease. These are:

•   Normal Pressure Hydrocephalus (NPH) – when there is a gradual buildup of cerebrospinal fluid (CFS) in the brain. This results in swelling and pressure which can damage brain tissue over time. Some of the symptoms present similar to dementia. CFS can usually be eased via a lumbar puncture to drain excess fluid.

•   Medications – some of the side effects or interactions of certain prescription drugs such as opiates (painkillers) and benzodiazepines (anxiety meds) as well as blood muscle relaxants and steroids can trigger cognitive symptoms. You must inform your physicians about every drug that you take.

Studies have shown that certain drugs may increase the risk for dementia, commonly found in Paxil, Benadryl, Clozaril, Oxytrol, and Tegretol).

• Depression – Severe depression has been found to cause symptoms of dementia. This is known as pseudodementia. After successful treatment of the depression, the cognitive impairment improves. Late-life depression however can be an early sign of Alzheimer's disease.

• Urinary Tract Infection (UTI) – Typical symptoms of UTIs, such as high fever or pain when urinating, are not usually present in older people. An older person may instead experience memory problems, dizziness, and confusion. Proper treatment of the UTI can help to ease the symptoms.

• Brain tumors and head injuries – tumors before they can be removed press on certain parts of the brain causing cognitive dysfunction. This can be reversed after removal. Traumatic brain injury can result in memory loss. Abnormal bleeding caused by a head injury can cause a buildup of pressure in the brain leading to dementia-like symptoms.

• Alcohol-related dementia – long-term, excessive consumption of alcohol can lead to health problems (like a damaged liver), ultimately causing cognitive impairment. Combining certain medications with alcoholic beverages can cause memory issues.

Getting Diagnosed

Should you be concerned about yourself or a family member possibly having a form of dementia, go for a complete medical workup as soon as possible. A physical exam and laboratory tests will help to spot early warning signs. There are many tests used nowadays to spot potential problems. These tests such as the Alzheimer's Disease Assessment Scale-Cognitive Subscale test measures memory, orientation, and language. The Folstein test or the Mini-Mental State Exam is a 10-minute questionnaire used to screen for dementia.

Although many cognitive tests, some of which can be done at home, are available, there is no single test that can diagnose dementia. They form part of the entire medical assessment. If you are already older and experience symptoms of dementia, you must find a good geriatrician or a doctor who has some experience with dealing with dementia.

Where to Find Help

In the US many nationwide programs offer information and helpful resources for Alzheimer's patients and their family members.

- The Alzheimer's Association, a voluntary organization offers care, support, and information. Their helpline is free and confidential, call 800-272-3900 to get reliable information from trained staff.

- Local organizations that are part of the Alzheimer's Association also provide a wealth of resources and do great work in treating, diagnosing, and researching dementia.
- AARP (aarp.org) is an organization that offers a wide variety of resources for people living with dementia and their caregivers.

Other good organizations to look up are Lou Ruvo Centre for Brain Health (Cleveland Clinic), the Dementia Action Alliance. The Family Caregiver Alliance, the Mayo Clinic's Alzheimer Disease Research Center, the Memory Disorders program at New York-Presbyterian/Weill Cornell Medical Center, the National Institute on Aging which funds Alzheimer's Disease research centers, and UCLA's Alzheimer's and Dementia Care Program which helps patients and families develop personalized plans.

Treatments

Early detection of dementia is critical to find ways to delay the progression of the illness and plan for the future. Proper care planning can help improve people's experience with dementia and can improve their quality of life.

Researchers and scientists are still working on ways to diagnose and treat dementia-related illnesses and Alzheimer's disease. Blood tests may soon be a possibility to screen people for possible signs. Treating dementia currently is difficult due to the complexity of the illness. Two drugs (cholinesterase inhibitors and anticholinergic medications) have been approved by the FDA to help lessen the symptoms of Alzheimer's disease but they come with their own side effects.

For now, treatment of dementia does not come in the form of a "superdrug", but rather in the quality of care and lifestyle plan. Each patient has to be treated individually because what works for one person may not necessarily work for another. Caregivers play an important role in this and the next chapter dwells more on this role.

Key Insights from this Chapter

1. Early detection of dementia is important to minimize its devastating effects.

2. Alzheimer's disease develops in three stages. These are mild (the early stage), moderate (the middle stage), and severe (the late stage).

3. There are plenty of resources on Alzheimer's and the various forms of dementia available to us.

4. Scientists and researchers have not yet found a curable treatment for dementia and Alzheimer's disease.

Identify Related Issues

1. Do you have persistent difficulty with your memory, cognition, or ability to perform everyday tasks or have you noticed this in a loved one?

2. Have you noticed a loved one become more anxious or confused or disorientated?

3. Are you worried that you or a loved one may possibly be in stage 1 of Alzheimer's disease?

Goals You Want to Achieve

1. To learn more about Alzheimer's disease and dementia so that:

   a. I have a better understanding of what cognitive decline is about

   b. I can make lifestyle choices now to protect against decline later

   c. I can plan for my future or the future of a loved one if diagnosed with dementia at a later stage in our lives.

Your Plan of Action

1. Make a note of symptoms that I or someone close to me exhibits.

2. Check with a medical practitioner if we should be concerned that these are symptoms of the early stages of dementia and not dementia mimics.

Action Checklist

1. When a family member or someone close starts exhibiting signs of cognitive decline, and even early symptoms Alzheimer's, we can sometimes find it hard to accept the truth and hence also have trouble moving on to the planning and caring stage. It is therefore important that we learn to regulate our own mindset and thinking. We can try to accept the notion that there is no single infallible entity in this entire universe. All things go through phases of decline, decay and eventual passing. This truth also applies to us humans. As we learn to accept and understand this truth, it can help us to cope with the mental stress.

2. If my family or I start to exhibit signs of dementia onset, we will research more about these symptoms and get information from reputable dementia organizations online or by visiting community groups/clinics or a geriatrician/medical practitioner to learn more before taking the next steps in caring and planning. It does no good to jump the gun by prematurely worrying. At the same time, on the other end of the spectrum, properly planned care system will go a long way in helping and boosting the quality of care for the afflicted.

Chapter 11 – Arranging Support and Care

Summary

In the final chapter of his book, Keep Sharp, Dr. Gupta discusses the financial and emotional aspects of caring for patients with Alzheimer's disease. He also discusses the toll it takes on caregivers, especially family caregivers.

Caring for a family member who has newly been diagnosed is very challenging. Family members are usually stressed about how they will be able to afford the care and whether their loved one will receive quality care in a safe environment.

Assisted care facilities

In the Netherlands exists an ideal assisted care facility, known as De Hogeweyk. Patients who have advanced dementia are catered for at this place which is like a little village. It is mostly funded by the Dutch government and is very different from the usual type of extended care facility.

In the true sense of the word, it is like walking into a beautiful village that looks like any other village with restaurants, salons, gardens, etc. It has been specifically designed so that people with extreme memory loss can live in familiar surroundings while still being secure. There are no wards and people from outside the village are encouraged to visit and make use of the facilities.

Staff are highly trained in the methods specific for handling people with dementia. Patients are encouraged to pursue any activities that keep their brains challenged. Hogeweyk is a great model for other countries to aspire to. Unfortunately, facilities like this do not exist anywhere else at present.

In the US the majority of people living with dementia live at home, cared for by family or friends. Spouses make up the largest portion of caregivers. According to Dr. Gupta, about "60 million Americans are caring for someone with Alzheimer's disease". This is a staggering number. Finding the right care and being able to afford a top assisted care facility is very difficult for most families. So, they often opt to take care of the patient at home.

You – the diagnosed

A dementia diagnosis is life-changing; for the individual and their loved ones. As soon as possible after your diagnosis, you need to find information and support for caregiving. Here's what you should do:

- Find a good support network in your local area so that you can learn more about the challenges ahead.
- Find an early-stage engagement program close to you. Many adult day health care centers, specializing in

serving dementia patients are opening up in many cities. They offer a wide variety of cognitive therapies.

- Find a clinical trial that you can participate in (should you want to participate in one).
- You will have to make a plan to keep your home safe especially for the later stages of the disease.
- Ensure that a proper legal plan is in place. You may need to draft a power of attorney and make sure there are adequate instructions in place regarding care etc. for the last part of your life. Look into what it means to get an advance directive, a living will, and a trust if required.
- You need to put a financial plan in place to make sure your finances are in order. Identify the cost of care and bring in a financial advisor if needed.
- Build a care team; identify and develop your care team. If you want to avoid a court-appointed guardian, discuss your options with family members as soon after diagnosis as possible.

You – the caregiver

Statistics show that often people who care for their spouses with dementia are "six times more likely to develop dementia than people in the general population". Caring for a loved one with dementia is very stressful and these caregivers are called the "invisible second patient".

In addition to this stress, the spouse caregiver often ends up being lonely, depressed, and inactive. Caring for a dementia patient with their changing moods, changing behaviors and other dementia-related symptoms is not an easy task.

If you are the primary caregiver who is taking care of a dementia patient, it is important you remember to take care of yourself as well. Be aware of your own diet, exercise routines, social connections with family and friends, and ensure you engage in activities that keep you challenged. Recruit help from others if you need it.

At the beginning of a dementia diagnosis, one of the hardest things that family members/caregivers go through is denial, which is normal. It is scary to watch a loved one go through the changes that cognitive decline entails. Together with this denial many people often feel guilt that they had not noticed the symptoms earlier and done something about it sooner. However, it is not easy to know the signs. The disease varies from patient to patient.

As a caregiver, you must try to connect with other caregivers who are in the same kind of situation. Sharing your experience with others often helps and you can share ideas and information as well. AARP and the Alzheimer's Association have a wealth of resources for caregivers to tap into.

Arming yourself with as much information as possible as soon as you can, will go a long way towards understanding what needs to be done after a dementia diagnosis is made.

Key Insights from this Chapter

1. The diagnosis of Alzheimer's and dementia has a big impact on family and friends.

2. Good assisted care facilities are expensive. Patients are most often cared for at home.

3. If you have been diagnosed, it is highly recommended you provide instructions for your future care and end of life.

4. Caring for a partner who has dementia is challenging. Carers also need to take care of themselves.

Identify Related Issues

1. Have you been diagnosed with dementia?

2. Do you have a care plan in place?

3. Have you made sure your personal, legal and financial matters are in order?

4. If you are the carer, are you fully aware or prepared for your role? Do you think you will require additional help?

Goals You Want to Achieve

1. As a diagnosed dementia patient, I want to get my matters in order while I still can.
2. As the caregiver of a dementia patient, I want to gather as much information as possible and ensure I have a support structure in place for myself. I will also not forget to take care of myself as the caregiver, both physically and mentally as it is now even more important to do so due to the fact that another person depends on me for daily living.

Your Plan of Action

1. Patient: Put into place asap a plan for medical care, care at home or a facility, finances, legal aspects such as trusts, and advanced directives for the future.

2. Caregiver: Work with family and friends and support groups to plan and prepare for the care of the patient and your own role.

Action Checklist

1. Make a list of places and resources where help is available in my local area for a future need that may crop up so we are prepared.

2. Ensure that as the primary caregiver, a member of my family or close friend has support and knows that they do.

3. Make a list of contacts you can rely on in times of emergency for you and/or your caregiver. Find out if they will be willing and able to assist when and if you require their additional assistance.

4. <u>Neither the patient nor the primary caregiver:</u> If a member of my family has dementia and is being taken care of by another member of the family, I must make it a point to watch for caregiver burnout.

Conclusion

Research and studies into finding better treatments and even a cure for Alzheimer's are ongoing. Other studies are researching the possibility of a vaccine that clears tangled beta-amyloid plaques to see if it has an impact on cognition and memory.

Dr. Gupta and others are hopeful that these and other studies will lead us to a better understanding of complex degenerative brain diseases, in the future. Hopefully, there are new therapies and solutions together with preventive treatments in store.

In the meantime, we can put into place lifestyle measures to make our brains sharper, keeping them healthy and resilient. After working through the exercises in this workbook, you should now be more equipped to take on this challenge. Keep in mind that:

"You can build a better brain at any age"
Dr Sanjay Gupta

May you be well and happy

Addendum

Answers to Action Checklist in Chapter 3

Brain Facts	True	False
The human brain once damaged cannot be healed		✓
As we age our cognitive functions inevitably decline		✓
Our brains are more resilient than we think	✓	
All memory lapses are a sign of cognitive decline		✓
The left brain and the right brain often work together to process many functions	✓	
Doing daily crossword puzzles are enough to prevent cognitive decline		✓
Our brain cells stop growing when we reach adulthood		✓
Physical movement helps maintain brain health	✓	
What we eat has an effect on our brains	✓	
It is possible to keep our brains sharp as we get older	✓	

.

Made in the USA
Monee, IL
17 September 2022

14177538R00069